Fanfare 1

PROGRESS BOOK   MADELINE McHUGH

My name's

_____.

This is my book.

OXFORD UNIVERSITY PRESS

1 Words and numbers

1 Match the names with the pictures.

I'm Theo.

I'm Maria.

I'm Morgan.

I'm Joe.

I'm Wizzy.

2 Draw your photograph and write your name.

Hello. I'm _____.

3 Colour and match the pictures with the words.

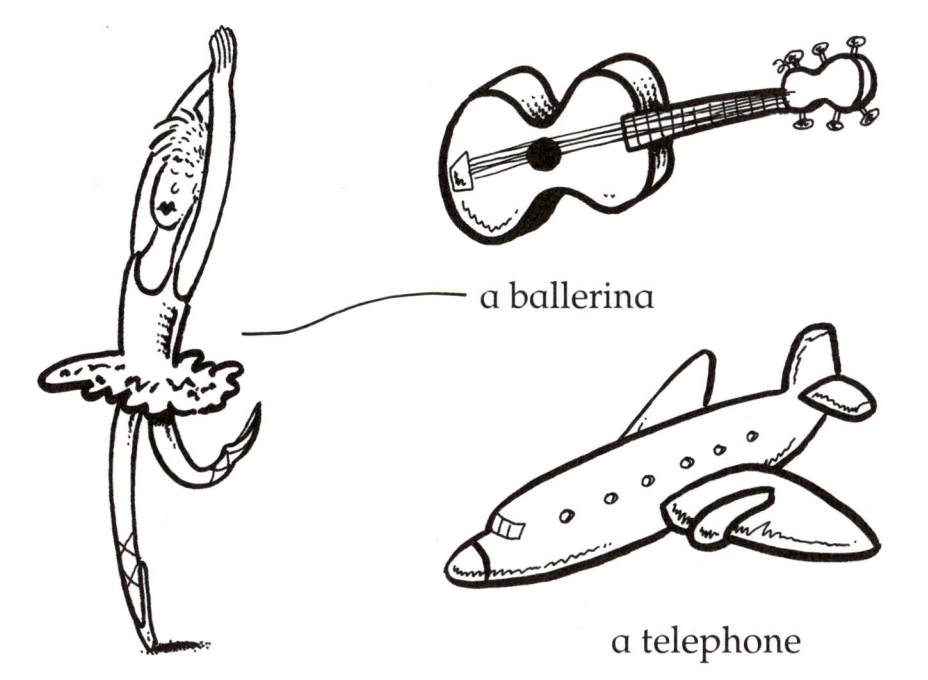

a jet

a ballerina

a robot

a telephone

a guitar

a computer

a taxi

a football

a photograph

a bus

4 Listen and write the numbers.

2 + 3 = 5   2 +   = 7

4 +   = 7   1 +   = 8

  + 4 = 5   + 1 = 10

  + 5 = 10   6 + 3 =

6 +   = 8   4 +   = 6

5 Match the words with the numbers.

one   six

two   seven

three   eight

four   nine

five   ten

More English words I know

pizza

cinema

cinema

coca-cola

hamburger

ZOO

Camping

Choose and colour a face.

Unit 1 was hard easy

2 Colours

1 Find the colours and colour the objects.

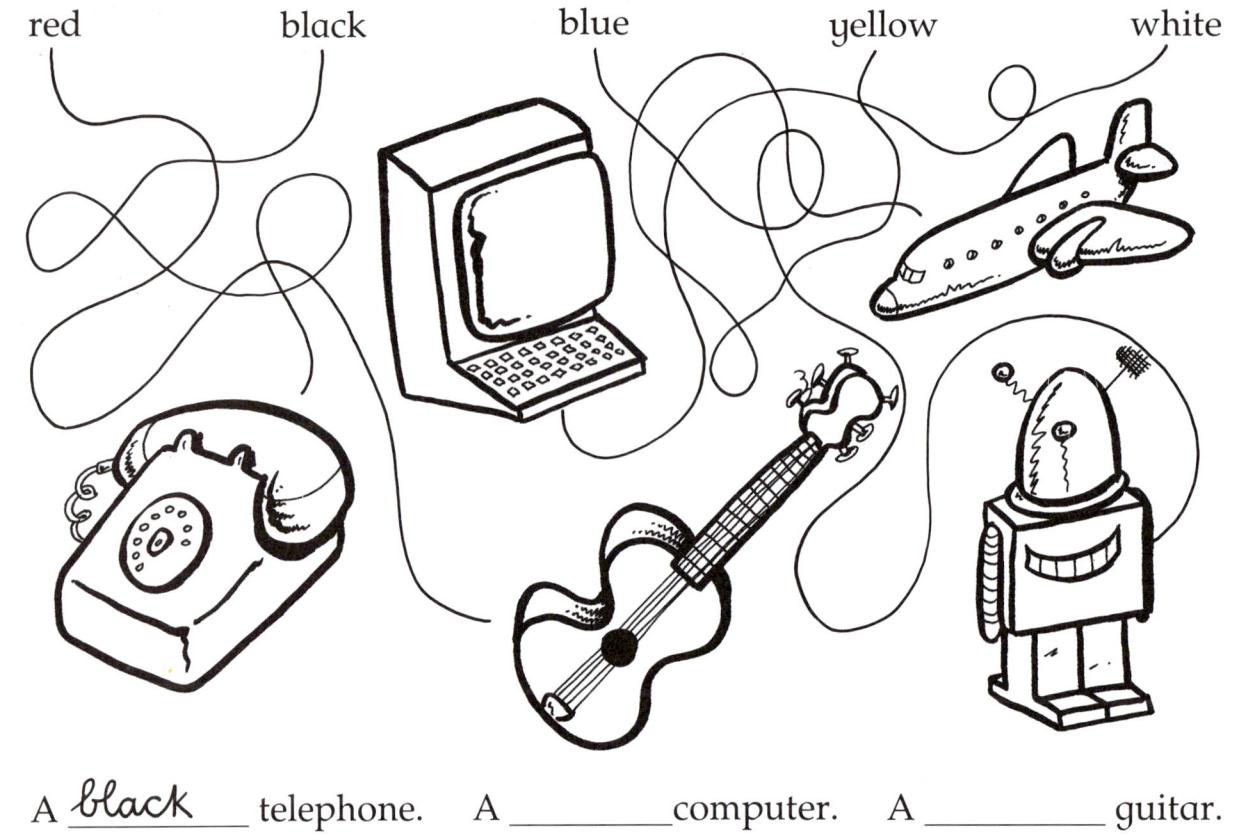

red   black   blue   yellow   white

A _black_ telephone.   A _____ computer.   A _____ guitar.

A _____ jet.   A _____ robot.

2 Listen and circle the colour word. Colour the objects.

A white /(black) taxi.   A blue / yellow train.   A red / blue bus.

3 Read and colour the paint pots.

green    black    yellow    pink    blue

red    purple    white    orange    grey

4 Write the answers and colour the numbers.

$2 + 4 = 6$
Red and blue is _purple_.

$2 + 3 = $ _____
Red and yellow is _____.

$3 + 4 = $ _____
Yellow and blue is _____.

$1 + 8 = $ _____
Black and white is _____.

$8 + 2 = $ _____
White and red is _____.

5 Colour and find the picture.

g = green   r = red   p = purple   b = blue   y = yellow   o = orange

What is it? It's a _____.

6 Find the colours in your class-room.

A green _____.   A pink _____.   An orange _____.

A grey _____.   A purple _____.   A red _____.

My colour collage

My colour collage is _____.

Unit 2 was hard easy

3 Shapes

1 Count the shapes.

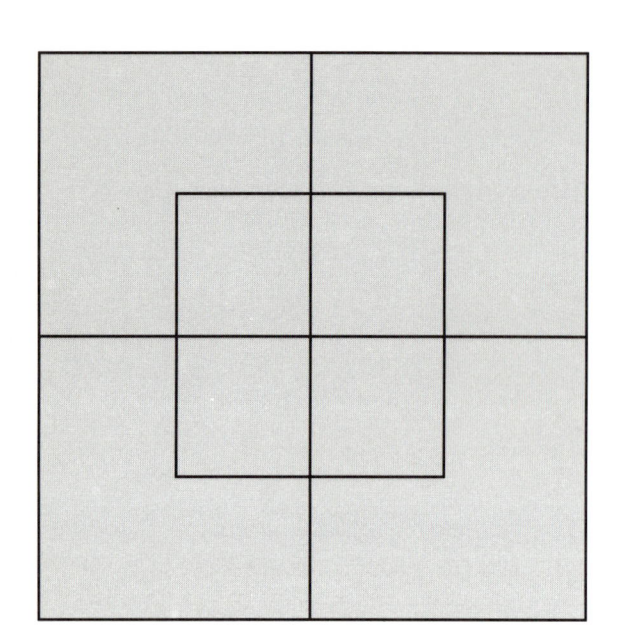

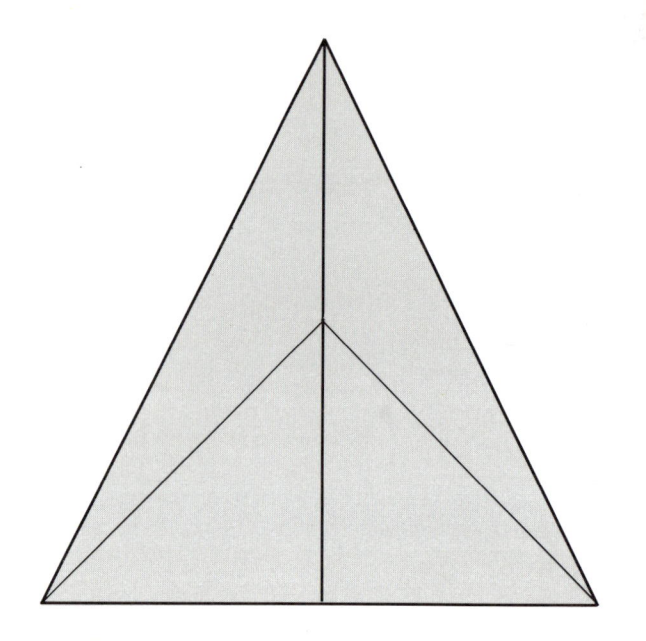

How many squares? ☐

How many triangles? ☐

2 Finish the patterns.

1. △ ☐ ○ △ ☐ ○ △ ☐ ○ △ ☐

2. ○ ○ △ ○ ○ ☐ ○ ○ △ __ __ __

3. ☐ △ ☐ △ ○ ☐ △ __ __ __ __

4. △ △ ○ ☐ ○ △ △ __ __ __ __

My shapes picture

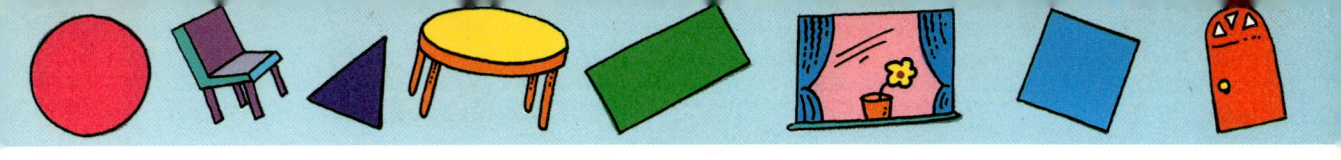

What is it? It's a _____ .

3 Listen and circle: *Yes* or *No*.

1 Yes (No)

2 Yes   No

3 Yes   No

4 Yes   No

5 Yes   No

6 Yes   No

4 Play Wizzy's game.

FINISH	34	33 Point to a	32	31 What is it?	30
24	25 Touch a	26	27 What is it?	28	29 Point to a
23 Touch a	22	21	20	19 What is it?	18
12	13 Touch a	14	15 Point to a	16	17
11	10 What is it?	9	8	7 Touch a	6
START	1	2 Touch a	3 What is it?	4	5 Point to a

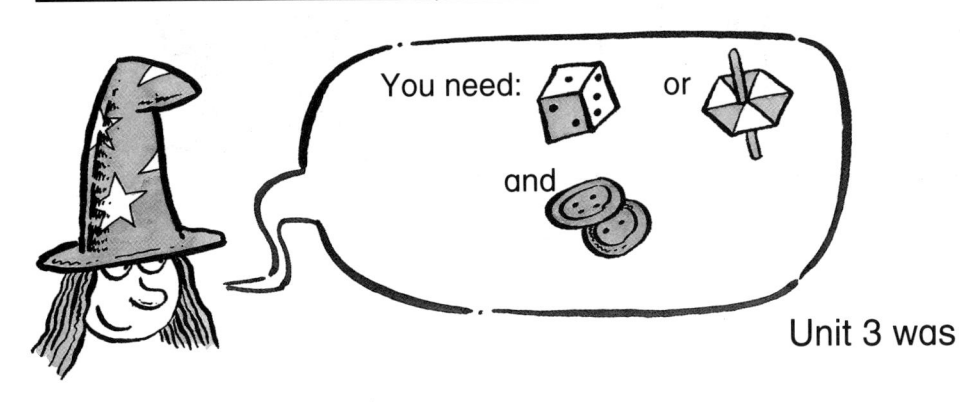

You need: 🎲 or 🔺 and 🪙🪙

Unit 3 was hard 😞 easy 😊

4 Where's the cat?

1 Match the words with the class-room objects.

a door

a table

a desk

a chair

a school-bag

a pencil

a box

a book

a window

a pencil case

a ruler

a computer

2 Find the differences.

3 Put the objects in the picture. Finish the sentences.

pencil

book

dog

My picture

The dog is_____the_____.

The book is_____the_____.

The pencil is_____the_____.

My friend's picture

The dog is_____the_____.

The book is_____the_____.

The pencil is_____the_____.

4 Listen and join the dots.

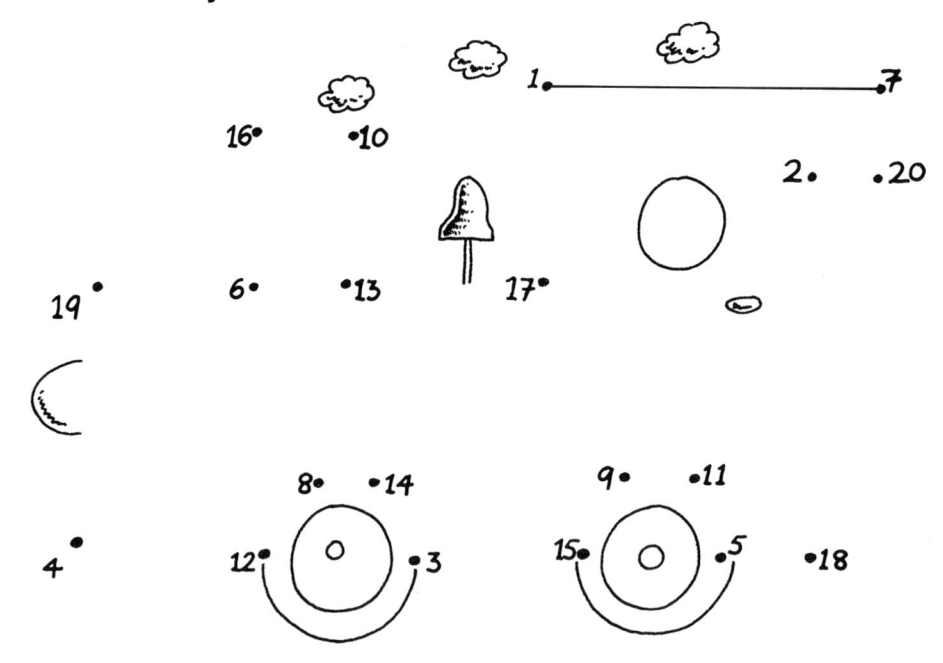

What is it? It's a _____.

5 Colour the numbers.

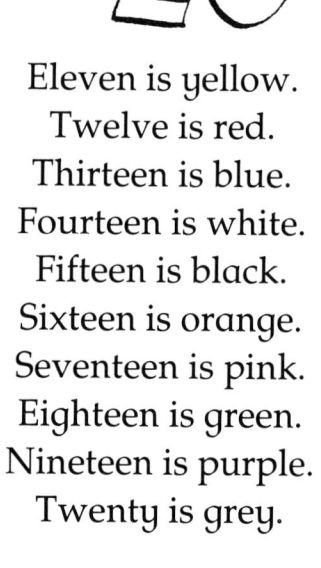

Eleven is yellow.
Twelve is red.
Thirteen is blue.
Fourteen is white.
Fifteen is black.
Sixteen is orange.
Seventeen is pink.
Eighteen is green.
Nineteen is purple.
Twenty is grey.

My frog

Unit 4 was   hard 😞   easy 😊   17

5 My body

1 Draw the monster and label the parts of the body.

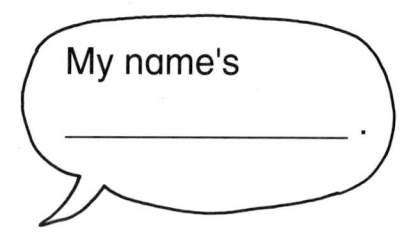

My name's _____.

head

hand

body

arm

leg

foot

toe

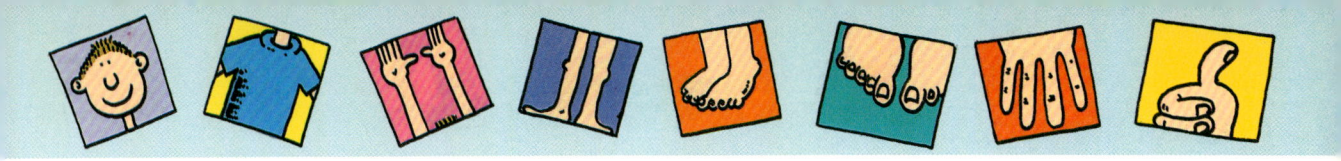

2 Read and colour the picture.

I've got...
a green body, a yellow head, blue legs, orange hands, and red feet.

3 Listen and number the monsters.

☐   1   ☐

4 Label the parts of the body.

head   body   arm   hand   finger   thumb   leg   foot   toe

head

5 Listen and circle: *Yes* or *No*.

1 Yes (No)   2 Yes No   3 Yes No
4 Yes No   5 Yes No   6 Yes No

My monster cards

Unit 5 was hard 😞 easy 🙂   21

6 My face

1 Label the face.

hair   eye   nose   ear   mouth

hair

2 Listen and number the faces.

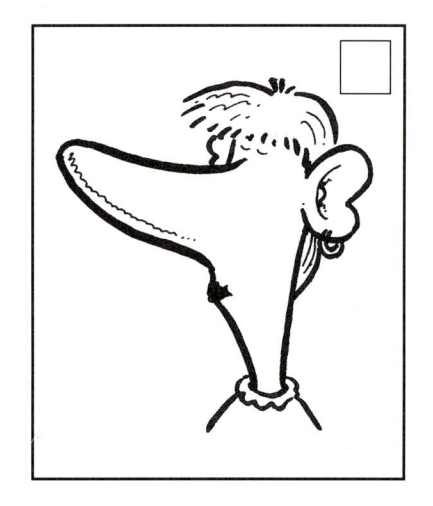

My mask

Hello. I'm _____. I've got _____ hair, a _____ nose, and a _____ mouth.

3 Find and circle the words in the right colour.

body words - red   transport words - black
face words - blue   class-room words - green

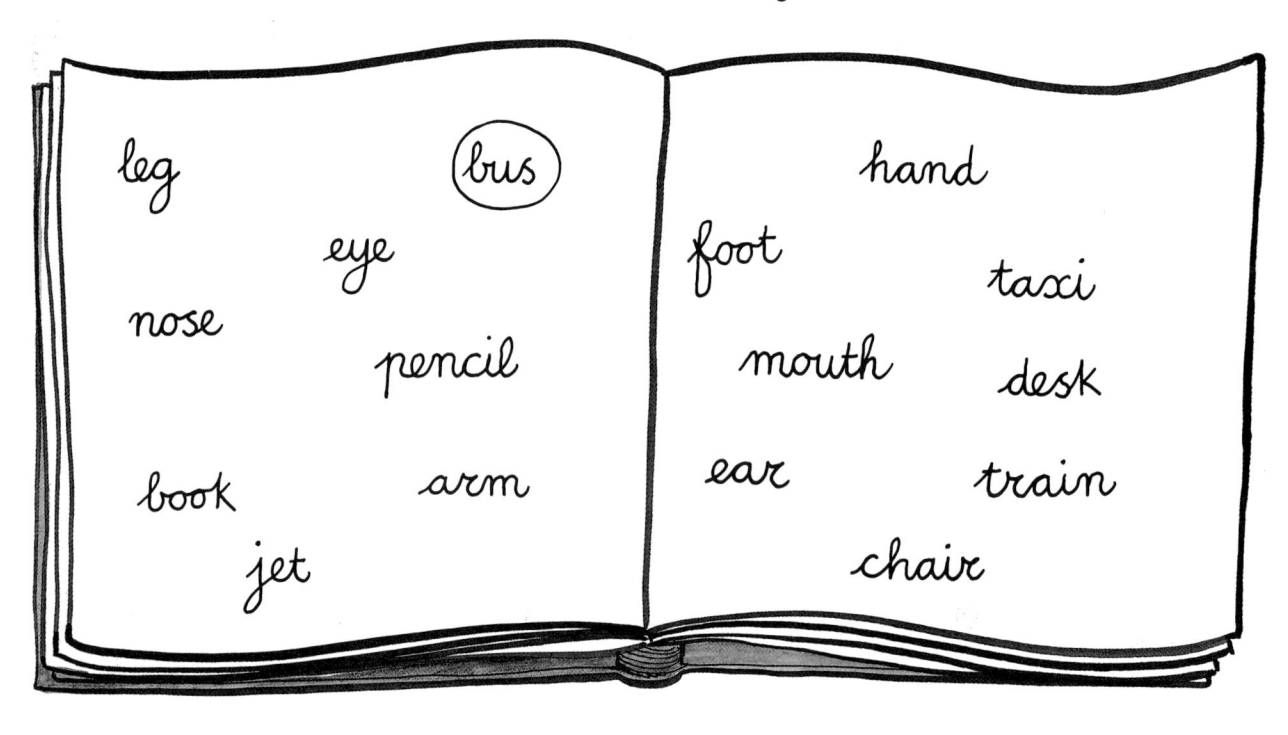

leg
bus
eye
nose
pencil
book
arm
jet
hand
foot
taxi
mouth
desk
ear
train
chair

4 Listen and circle: *Yes* or *No*.

WANTED

REWARD $5,000

1	Yes	No
2	Yes	No
3	Yes	No
4	Yes	No
5	Yes	No

5 Make a table for your class.

Hair				Eyes		
black	brown	blonde	red	blue	brown	green

6 Make graphs for your class.

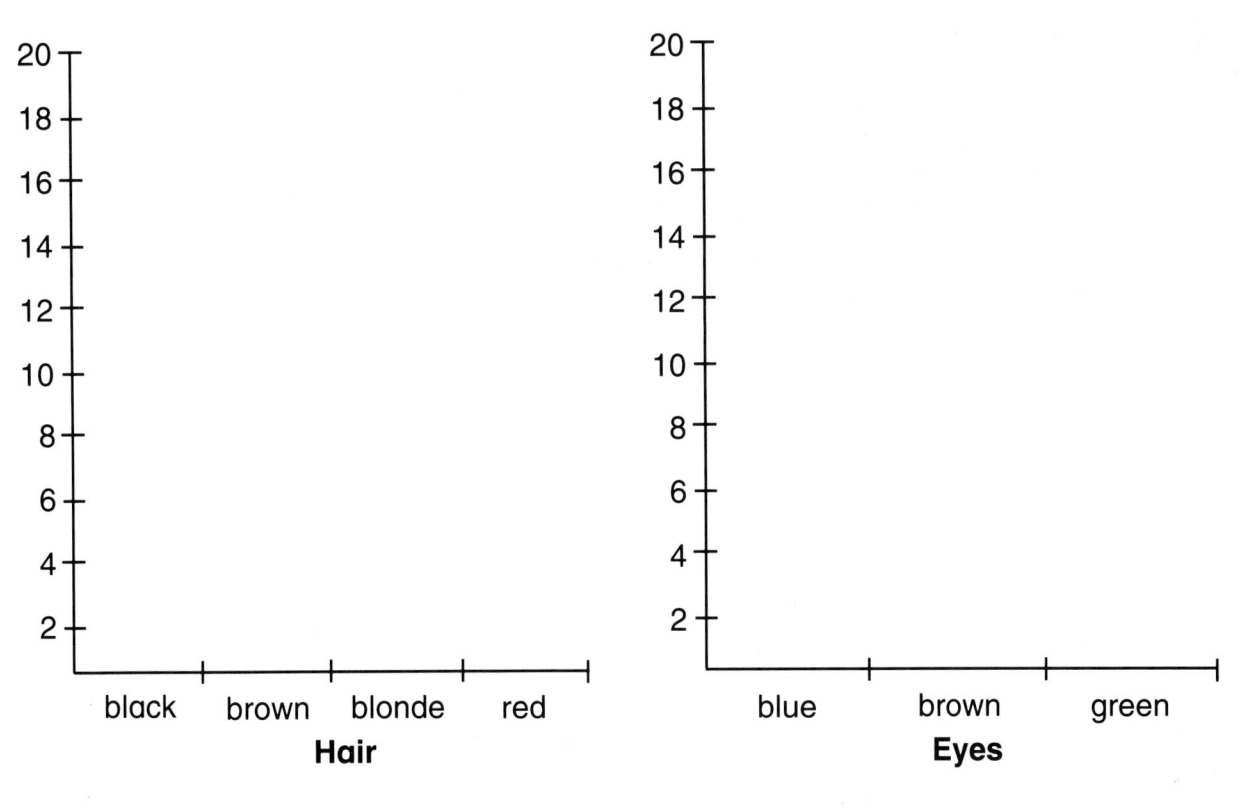

Hair

black brown blonde red

Eyes

blue brown green

Unit 6 was

7 My family

1 Look and circle the right word.

1 He's Theo's (grandad)/grandma.
2 She's Theo's grandma/mum.
3 He's Theo's dad/brother.
4 She's Theo's mum/sister.
5 She's Theo's brother/sister.
6 He's Theo's brother/dad.

My family album

2 Write about Joe and Wizzy.

Name	Country	Age	Brothers	Sisters
Joe	Britain	8	1	1
Wizzy	Vangland	13	2	2

His name's ___Joe___.
He's from _____.
He's _____.
He's got ___ _____
and ___ _____.

Her name's _____.
She's from _____.
She's _____.
She's got ___ _____
and ___ _____.

3 Write about your friends.

Name	Country	Age	Brothers	Sisters

His name's _____.
He's from _____.
He's _____.
He's got ___ _____
and ___ _____.

Her name's _____.
She's from _____.
She's _____.
She's got ___ _____
and ___ _____.

4 Do a class survey.

5 Draw and write about your home.

_____ people live in my home. _____

_____ and me.

Unit 7 was   hard   easy

8 Happy birthday

1 Make a calendar.

January	F_____	M_____
A_____	M_____	J_____
J_____	A_____	S_____
O_____	N_____	D_____

March   October   June   April   December   September
January   August   May   July   November   February

2 Ask your friends: *When's your birthday?* Write the names.

Month	Name	Month	Name
January		July	
February		August	
March		September	
April		October	
May		November	
June		December	

3 Add the numbers and write the ages.

How old are you?

I'm _____.

How old are you?

I'm _____.

How old are you?

I'm _____.

4 Write the sentences.

1 younger | I'm | . | than | Wizzy

   I'm younger than Wizzy.

2 Maria's | . | than | older | Joe

   _____

3 ? | old | you | How | are

   _____

4 ten | . | I'm

   _____

5 in | My | November | . | birthday's

   _____

5 Draw and write about you and your friends.

[   ]   me   [   ]

I'm older than _____.   I'm younger than _____.

32

My birthday card

Unit 8 was hard / easy

9 Food

1 Do the food crossword.

1 ↓ b
2 → i
3 → s
4 → c
5 → u
6 → i
7 → t
8 → s

2 Draw more hot and cold foods.

3 Listen and draw the faces.

4 Finish the questions and ask your friend. Circle: *Yes* or *No*.

		Me	My friend
Do you like ____ ?		Yes No	Yes No
Do you like ____ ?		Yes No	Yes No
Do you like ____ ?		Yes No	Yes No
Do you like ____ ?		Yes No	Yes No
Do you like ____ ?		Yes No	Yes No
Do you like ____ ?		Yes No	Yes No

5 Match and write the days of the week.

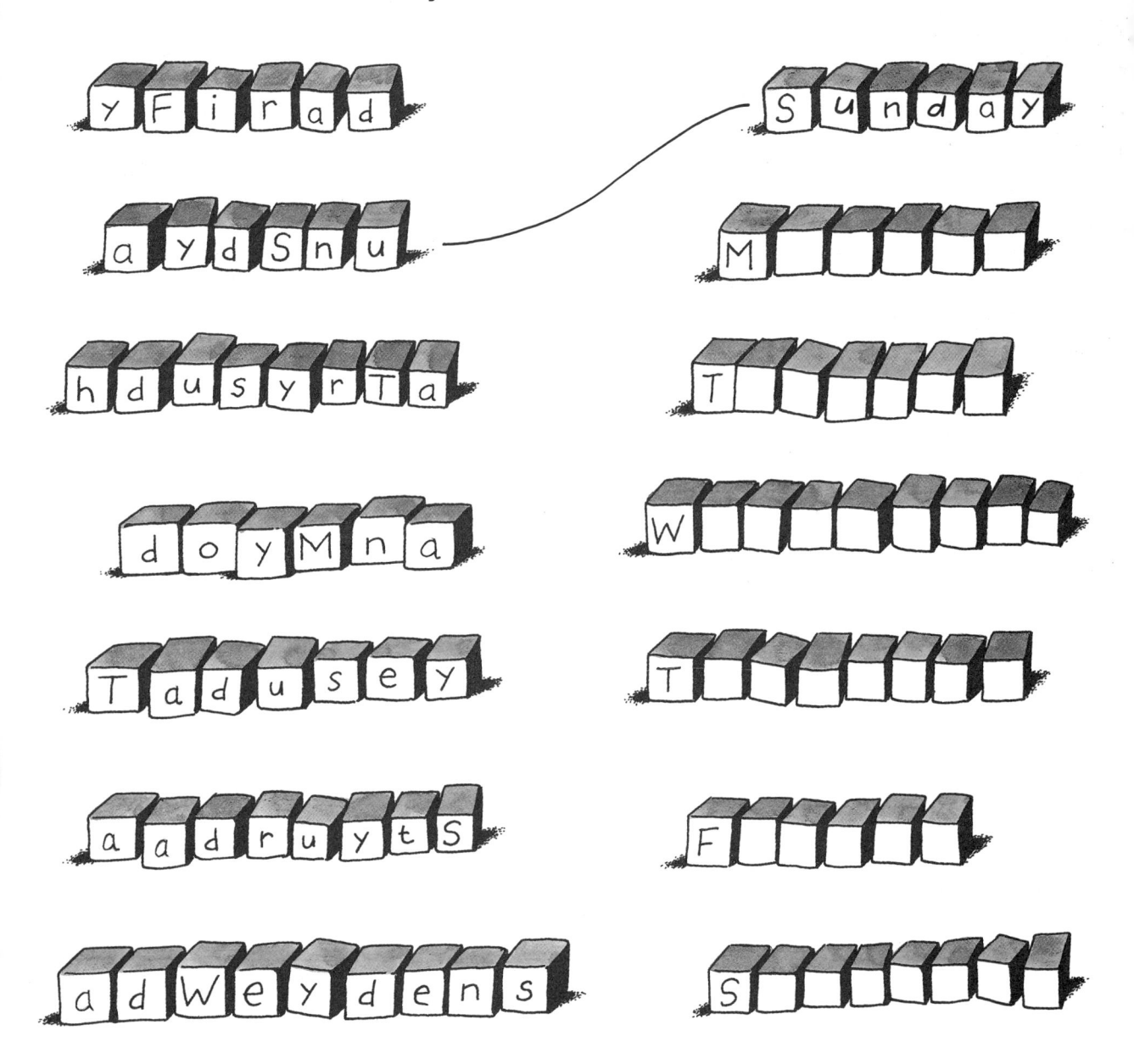

yFirad — Sunday

aydSnu — M_____

hdusyrTa — T_____

doyMna — W_____

Tadusey — T_____

aadruytS — F_____

adWeydens — S_____

6 Finish the table.

Food		Days of the week		Colours	
I like	I don't like	I like	I don't like	I like	I don't like

My food diary

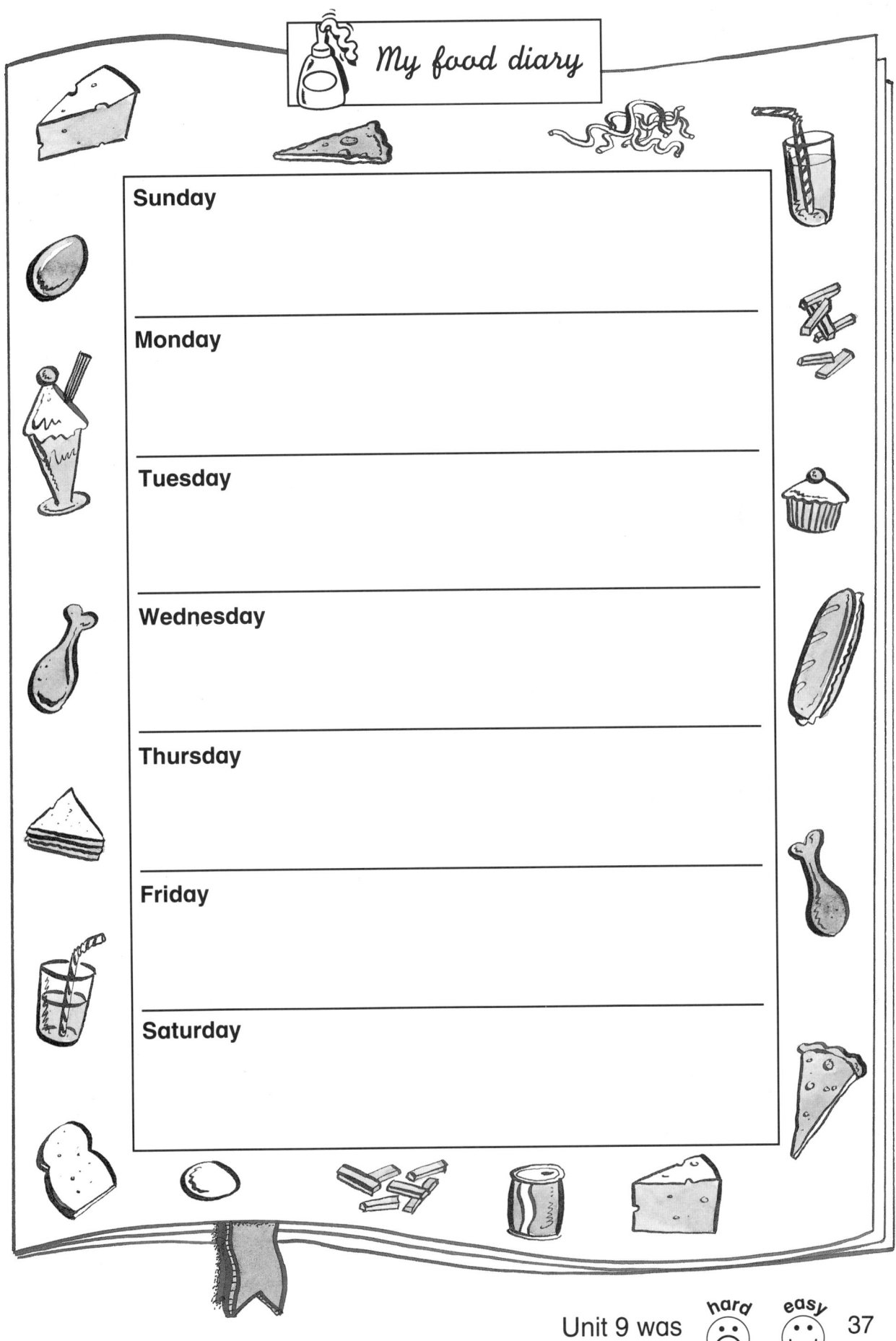

Sunday

Monday

Tuesday

Wednesday

Thursday

Friday

Saturday

Unit 9 was   hard / easy

10 Actions I can do

1 Look and label the pictures.

swim sing dance whistle jump play the guitar

dance

2 Finish the sentences about you.

I __can't__ fly.
I _____ dance.
I _____ swim.
I _____ sing.
I _____ wink.
I _____ play the guitar.

3 Finish the table for you and your friend. Write: *Yes* or *No*.

Can you ...?					
Me					
My friend					

4 Look at your picture dictionary and test your friend.

Can you say this in English?

Yes. Door.

Me	My friend
Points	Points
Total	Total

5 Choose the right sentence and finish the dialogue.

> I can click my fingers! I can whistle...　　Morgan, you can fly with me!
>
> One, two, three!　　I can't click my fingers.　　I can't whistle.

Wizzy: What's the matter, Morgan?
Morgan: I can't click my fingers.

Morgan: _____
Wizzy: Yes, you can, Morgan.

Wizzy: Abracadabra, abracadee! _____
_____.

Morgan: Look! _____
_____.

Morgan: ... but I can't fly.

Wizzy: Abracadabra, abracadee! _____
_____.

My board game

You need: 🎲 or 🎱 and 🍪

Unit 10 was hard 😞 easy 😊

11 Animals

1 Find the animal words.

d og

f _____

m _____

d	o	g	z	c	m	q
p	h	j	f	r	o	g
r	c	s	t	w	u	a
k	n	a	b	c	s	r
v	b	a	t	f	e	m
y	b	i	g	p	l	t
s	n	a	k	e	x	y

c _____

b _____

s _____

f _____

2 Say and match the rhyming words.

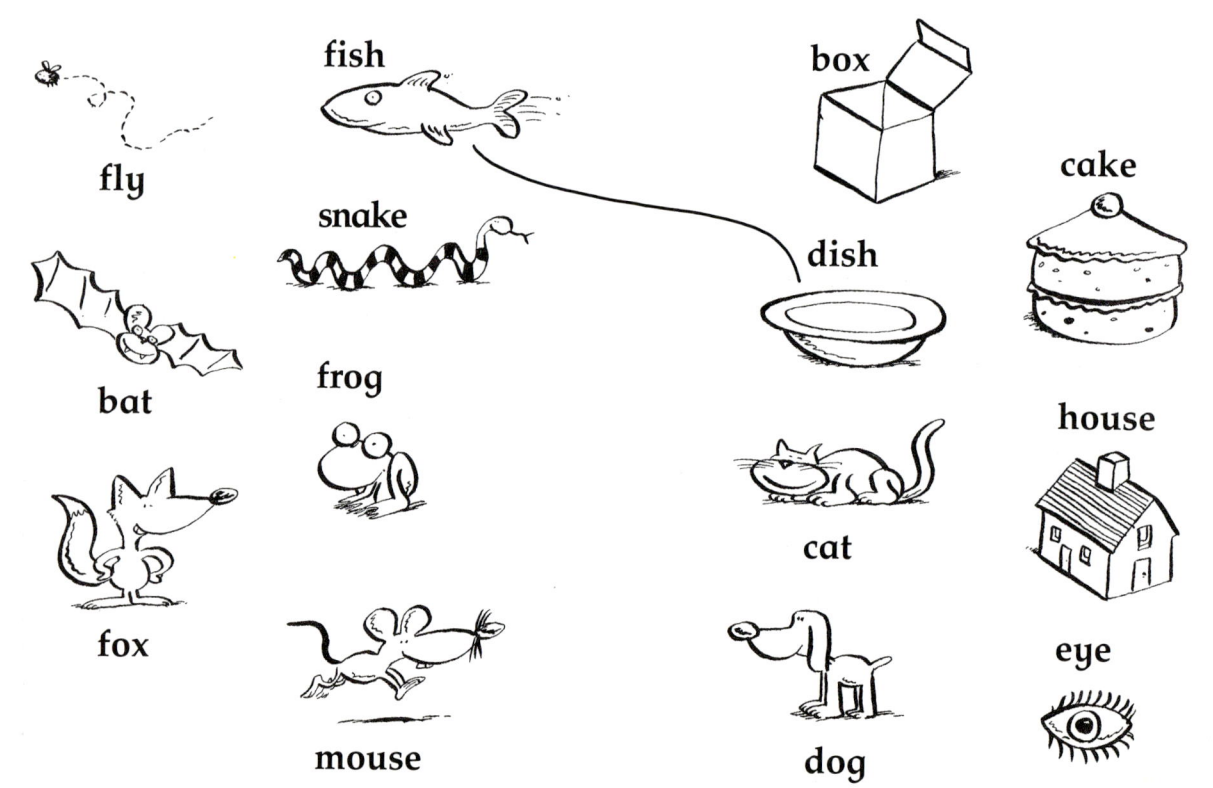

fly

bat

fox

fish

snake

frog

mouse

box

dish

cat

dog

cake

house

eye

42

3 Finish the sentences about the animals.

I can see...

a fox __on a table_____ .   a dog _____.

a bird _____ .   a mouse _____.

a tortoise _____ .   a rabbit _____.

4 Finish the table.

Hairy animals	Scary animals	Cold animals	Wet animals	Animals I like	Animals I don't like
dog					

5 Listen and number the animals.

6 Find the mystery word.

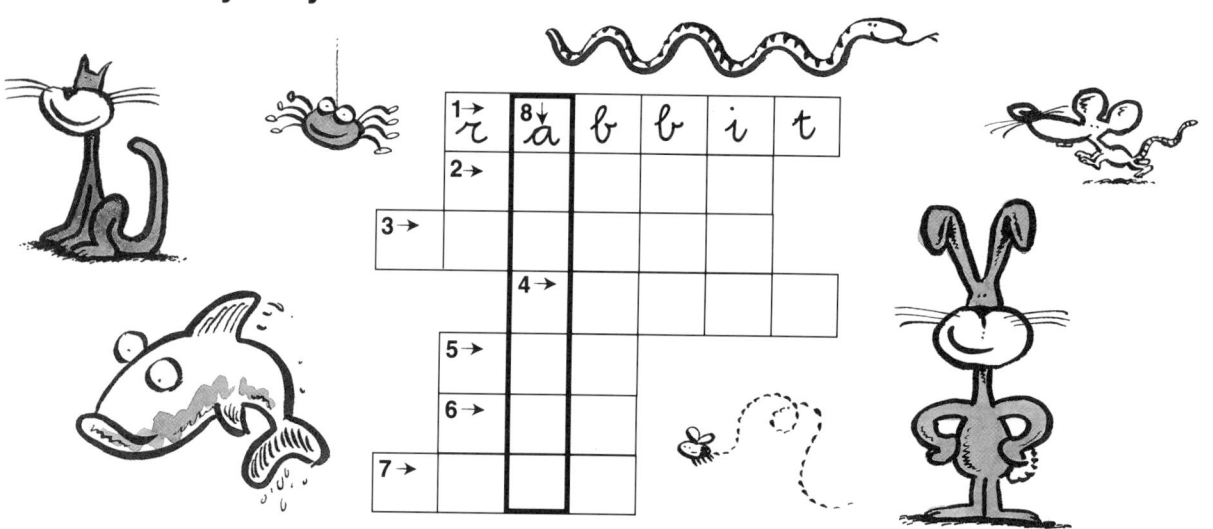

1. r a b b i t
2.
3.
4.
5.
6.
7.

1 It's hairy. It's got a short tail and big ears.
2 It hasn't got legs. It can't run and it can't fly. It's scary.
3 It's got eight legs. It can't fly.
4 It's small and hairy. It's got a long tail.
5 It's Wizzy's pet.
6 It's small. It's got wings and six legs.
7 It hasn't got legs. It can swim.

The mystery word is _____.

My mystery pet

Unit 11 was   hard   easy

12 Merry Christmas

1 Match the words with the presents.

- a doll
- a walkman
- a ball
- a kite
- a book
- a train
- a bike
- a jigsaw
- a tennis racket

2 Read Joe's letter.

> Dear [Father Christmas],
>
> For Christmas I want a [ball] and a [train].
>
> Have you got a [kite], please?
>
> Thank you.
>
> Merry Christmas and a Happy New Year.
> From
> Joe.

3 Write a letter to Father Christmas.

> Dear Father Christmas,
>
> For Christmas I want a   , a   , and a   .
>
> Have you got a   , please?
>
>   .
>
> Merry   and a Happy   .
> From
>   .

Unit 12 was

My picture dictionary

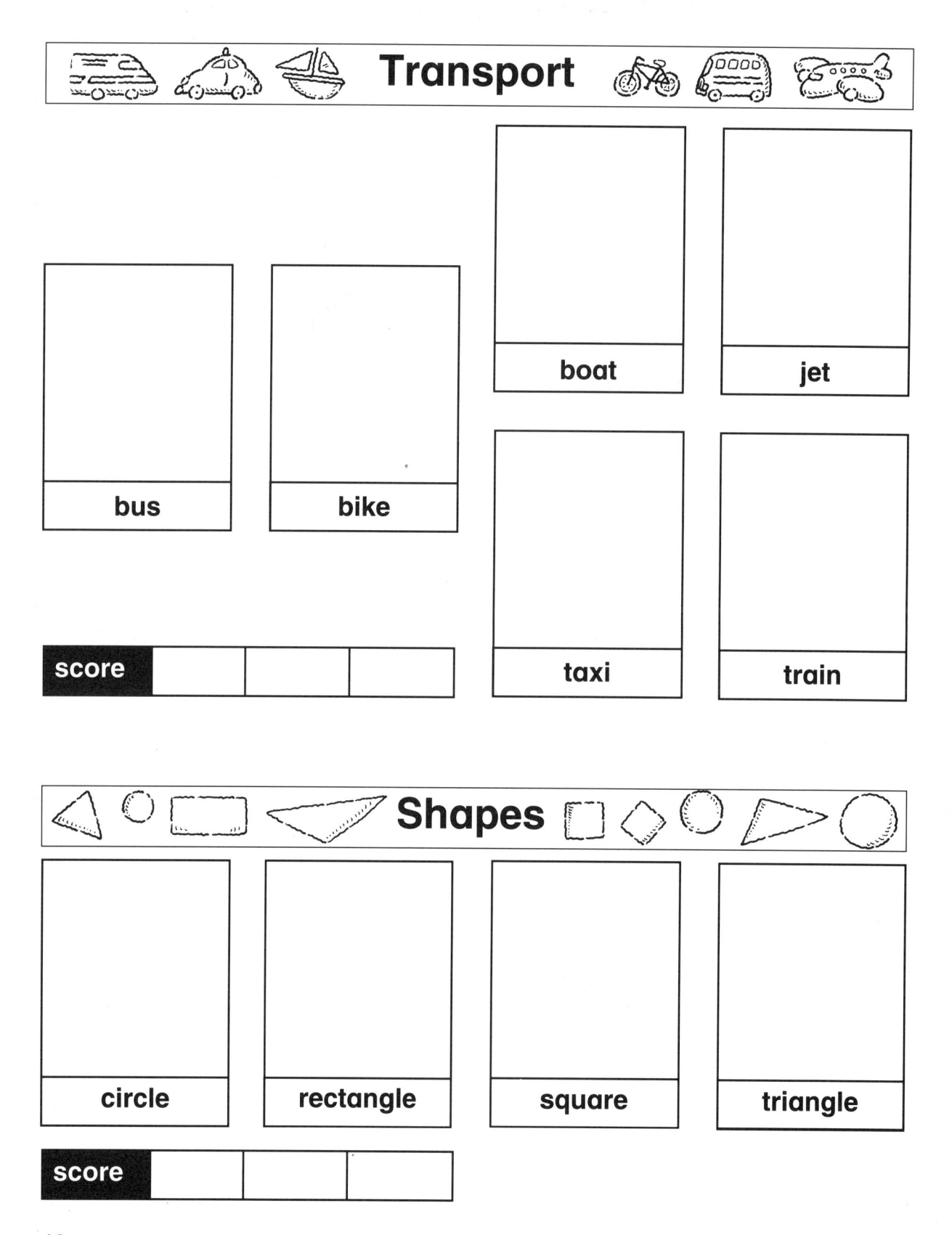

Transport

bus	bike

boat	jet
taxi	train

score

Shapes

circle	rectangle	square	triangle

score

48

Class-room

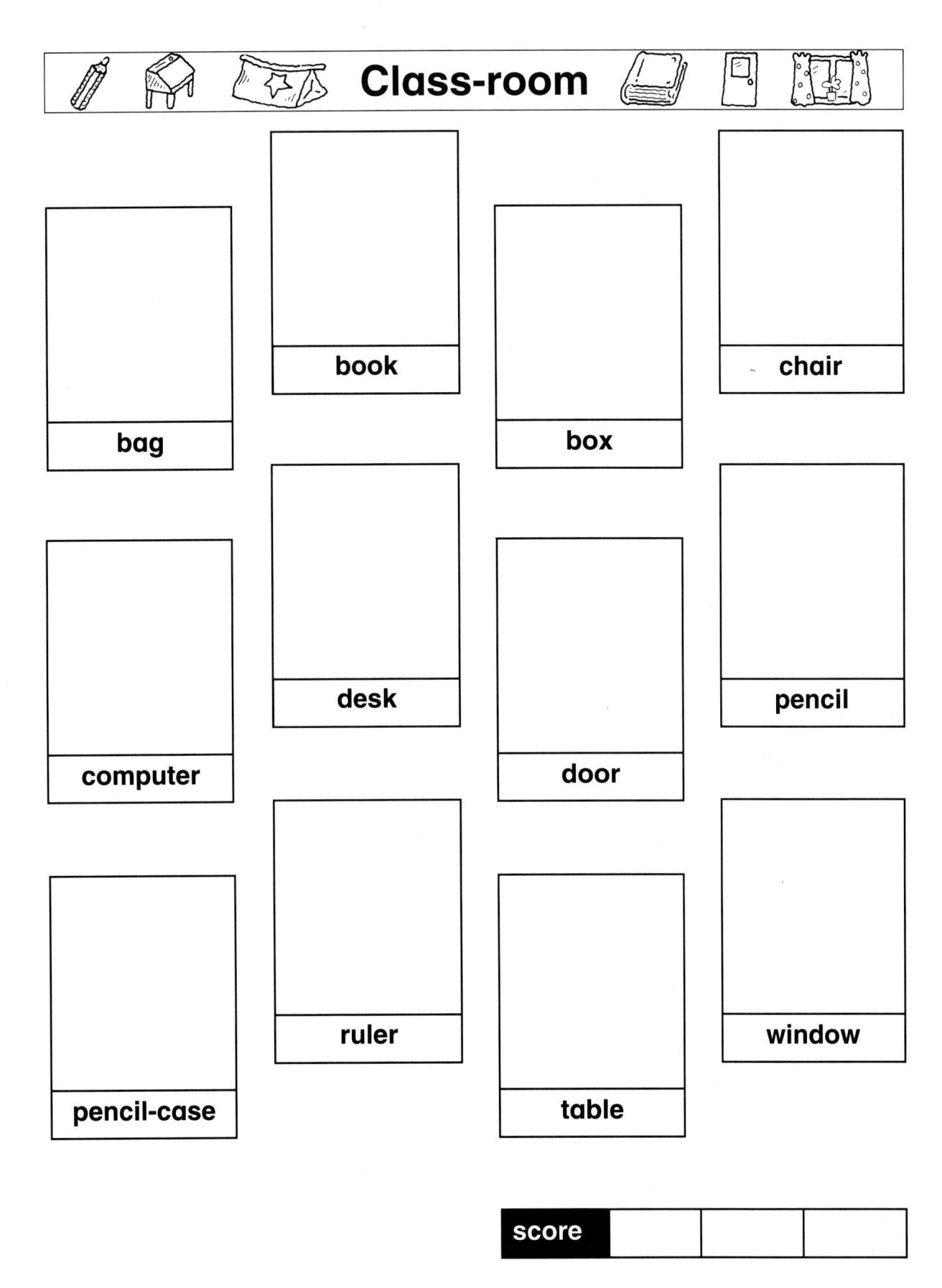

bag	book
box	chair
computer	desk
door	pencil
pencil-case	ruler
table	window

score

Body

arm	finger	foot	hand
head	leg	thumb	toe

score

Face

ear	eye	mouth	nose

score

Family

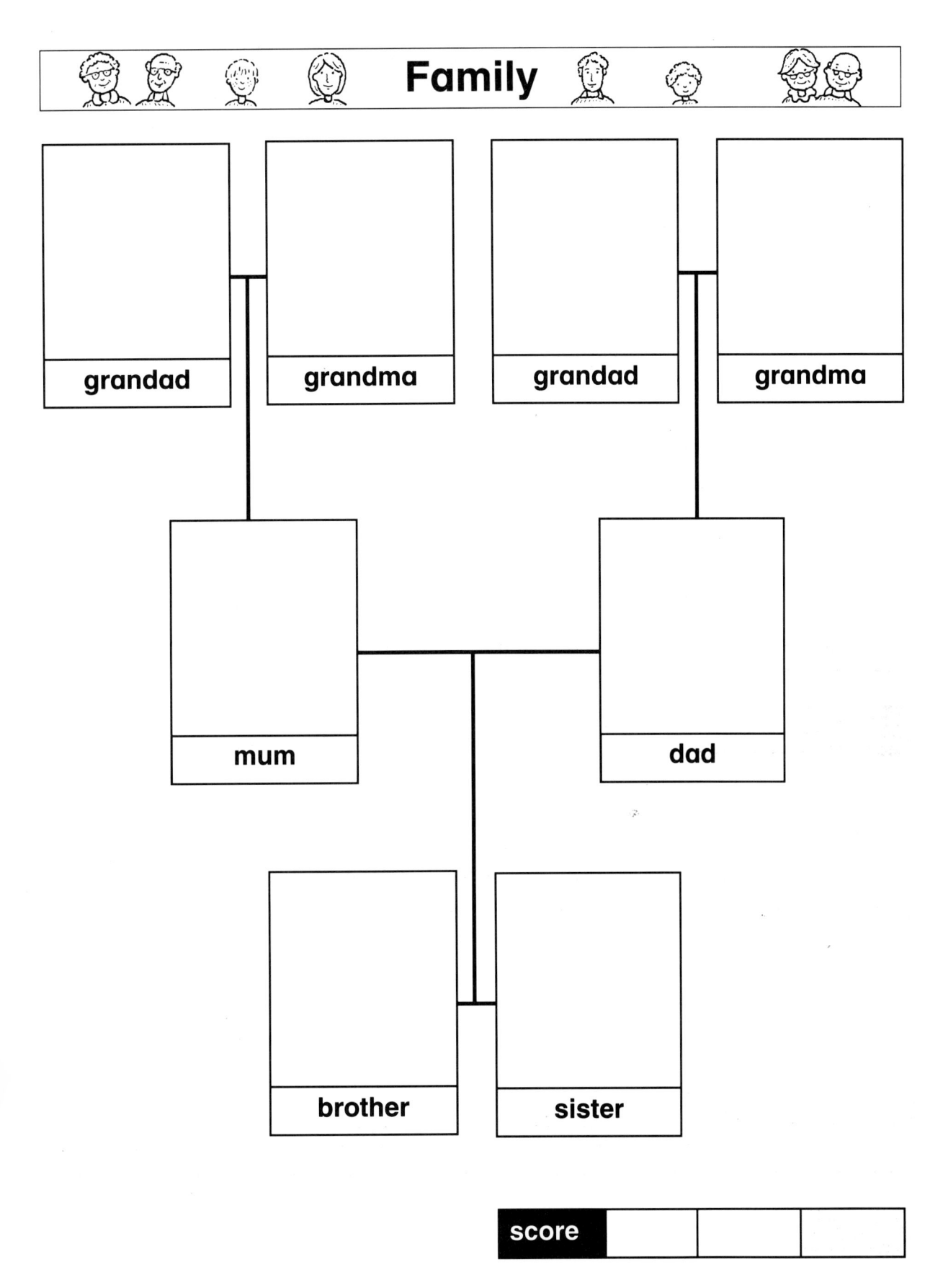

grandad	grandma	grandad	grandma

mum — dad

brother — sister

score

Food

biscuit	bread	cheese	chicken
chips	chocolate	egg	fish
ice-cream	salad	soup	steak

score

Actions

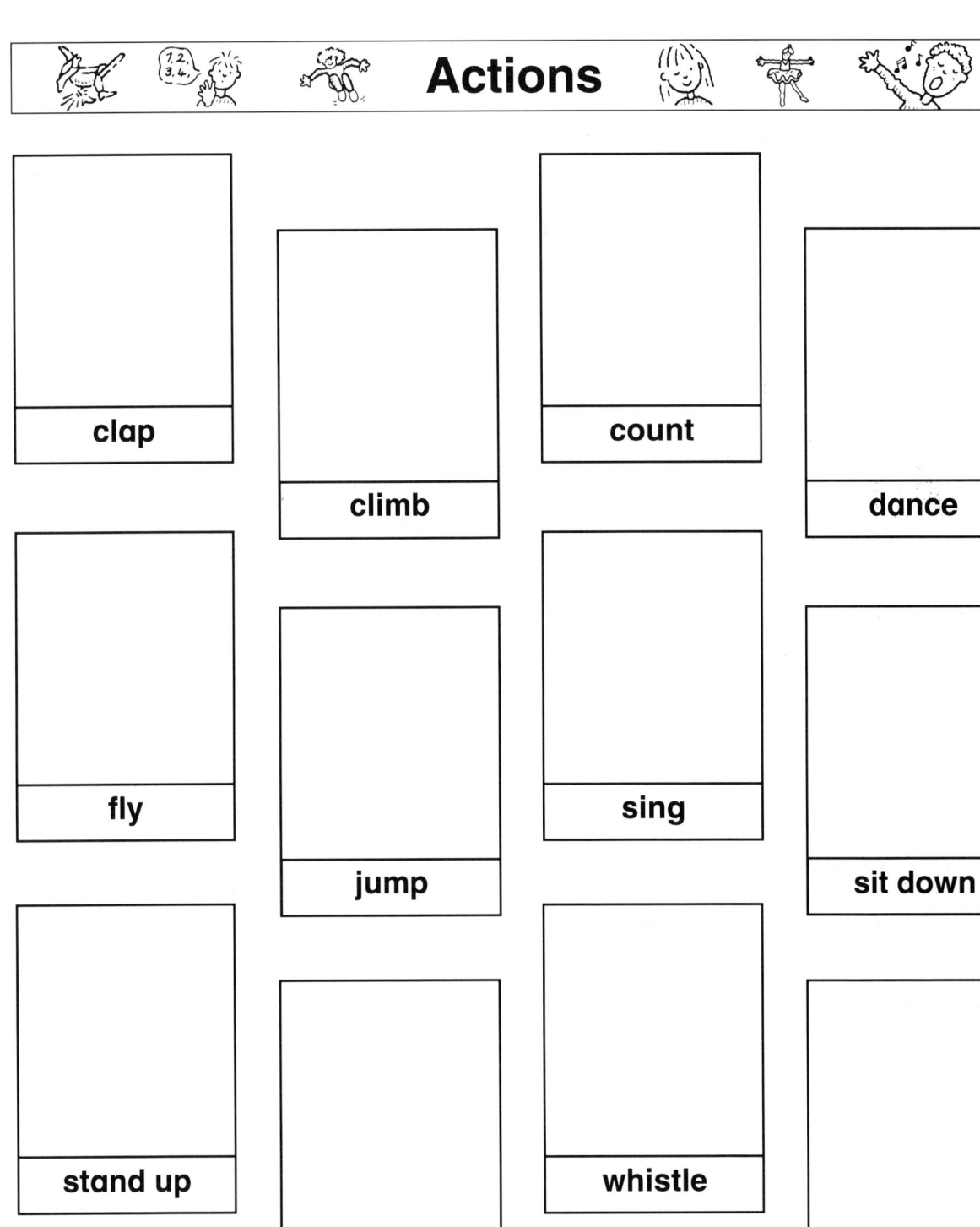

clap	
	climb
count	
	dance
fly	
	jump
sing	
	sit down
stand up	
	swim
whistle	
	wink

score

Animals

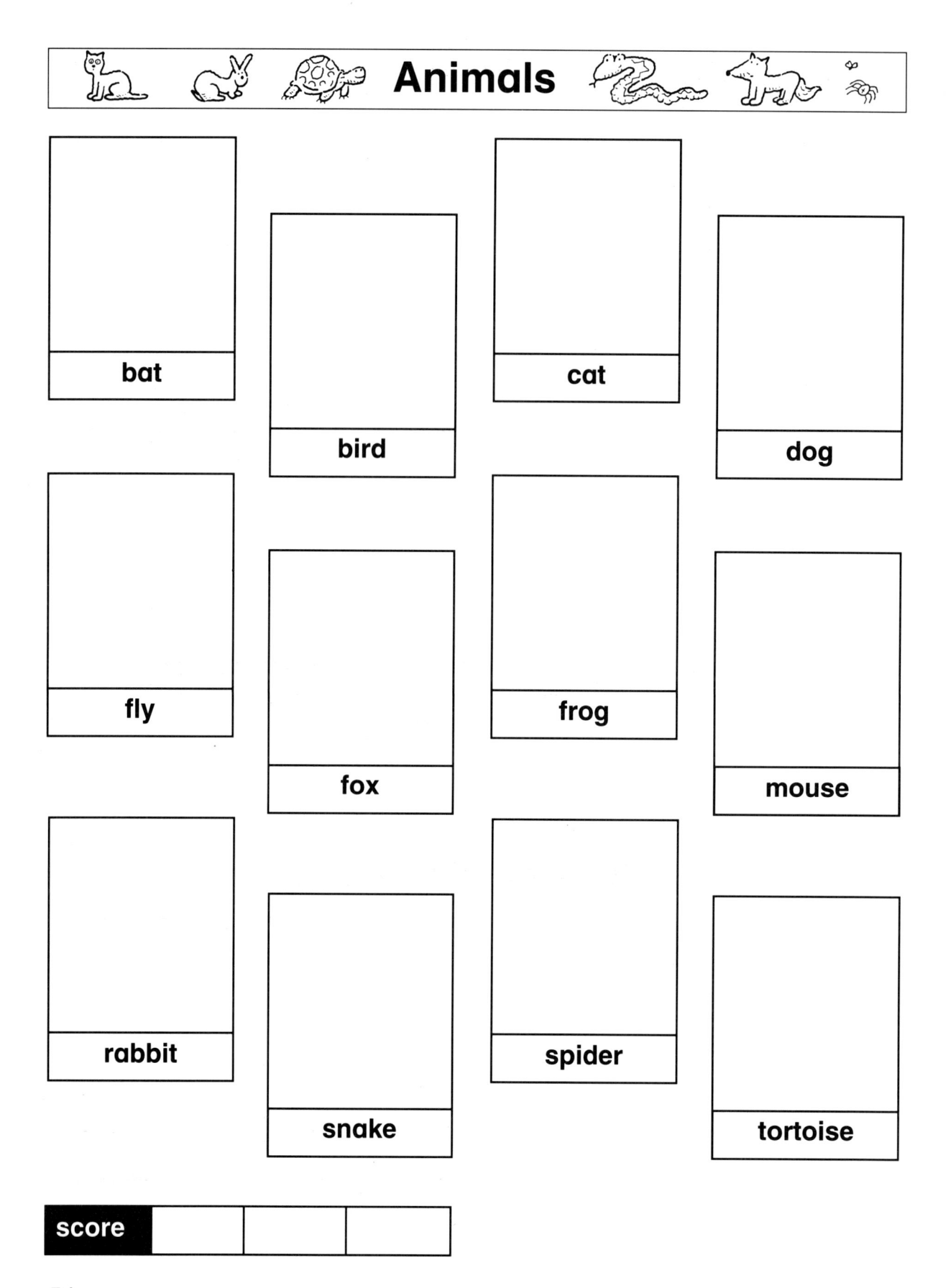

bat	
	bird
	cat
	dog
fly	
	fox
	frog
	mouse
rabbit	
	snake
	spider
	tortoise

score

Toys

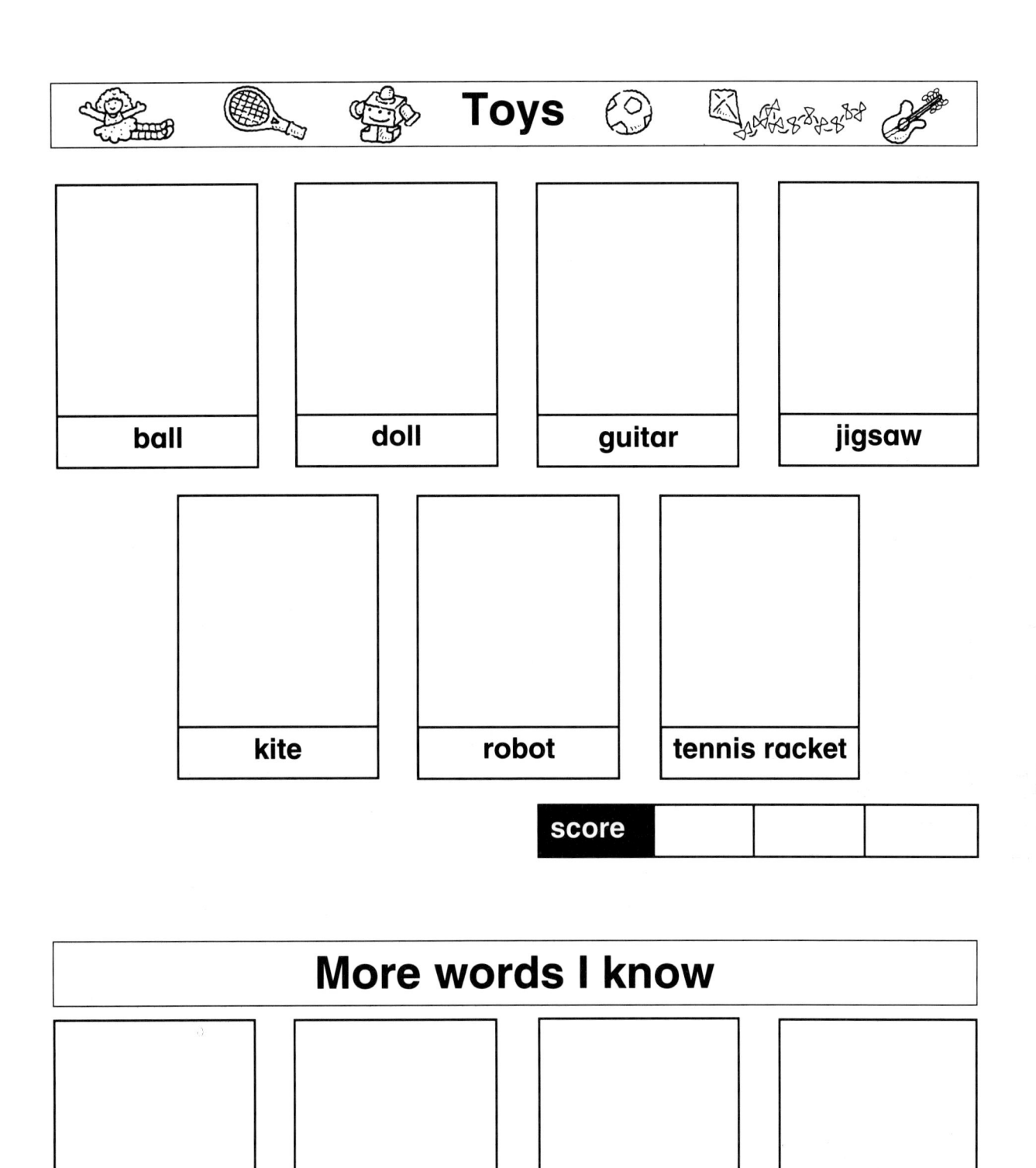

ball	doll	guitar	jigsaw

kite	robot	tennis racket

score

More words I know

55

58
- - - cut

- - - - cut
· · · · · fold

59

- - - cut

cut

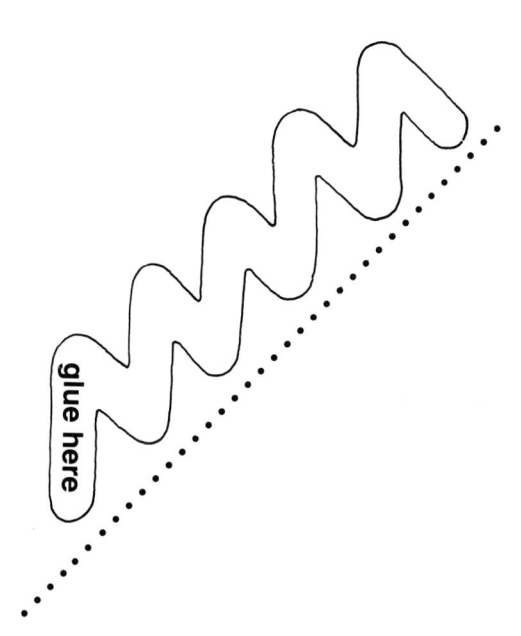

glue here

glue here

- - - - cut

...... fold

- - - - - cut

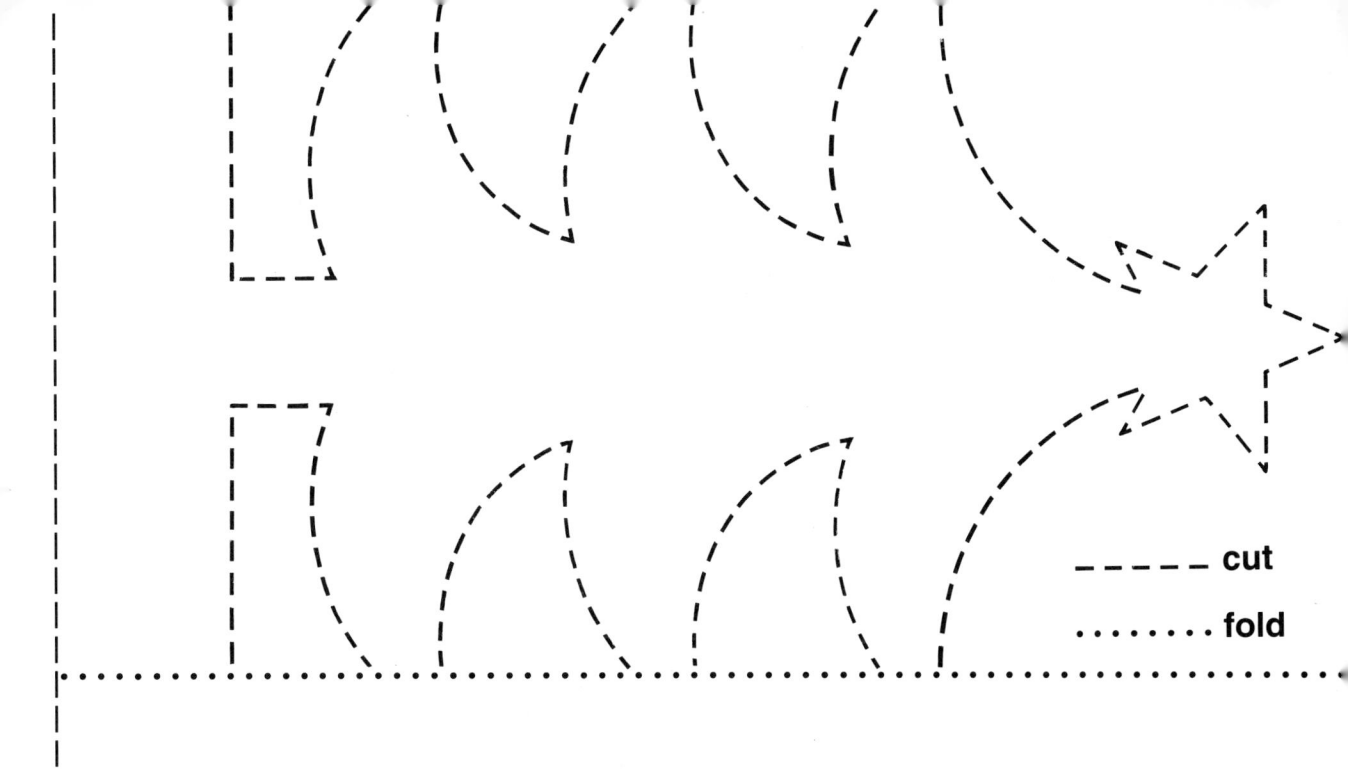

.... fold

67

70

71

74

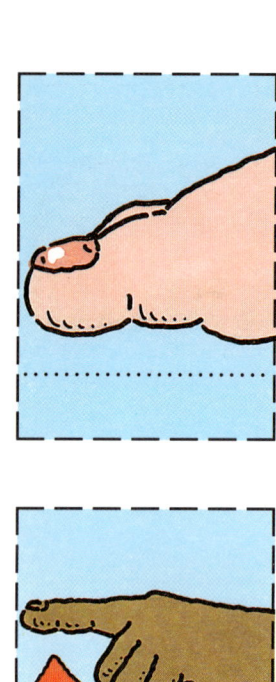

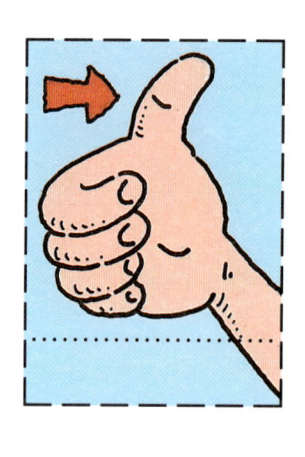

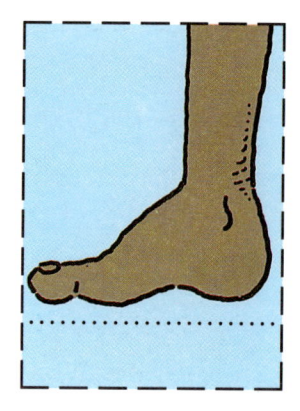

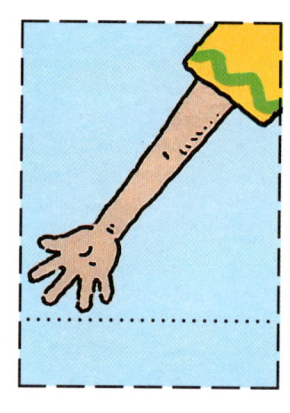

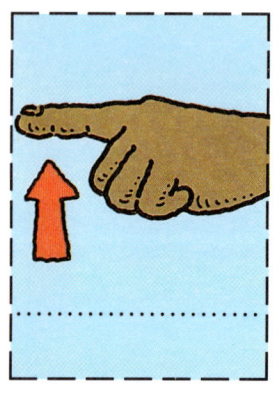

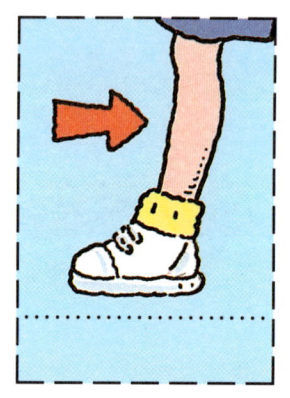

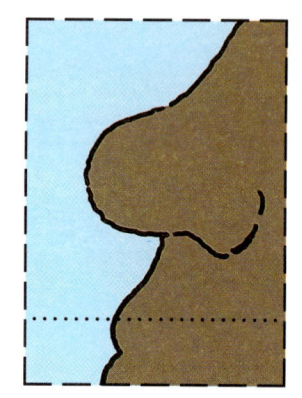

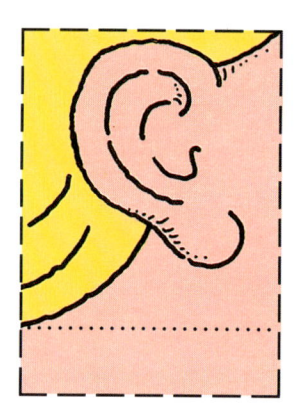

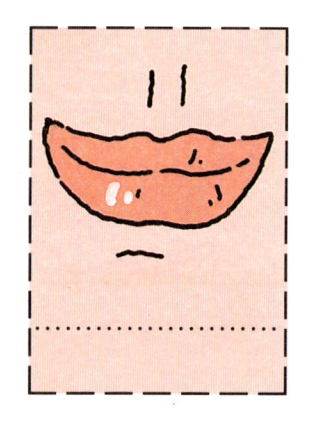

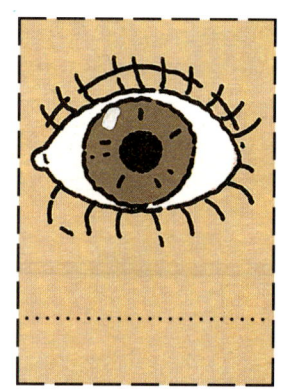

75

78

79

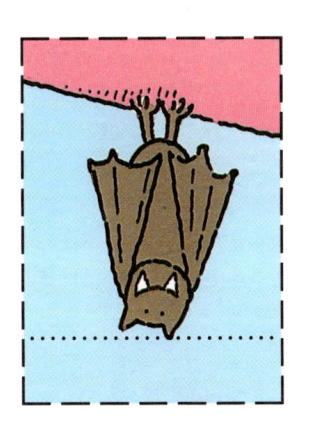

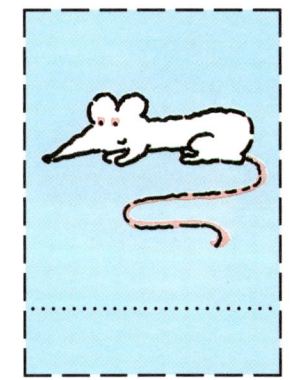